TUNING UP
A Visit with Eric Kimmel

by
Eric A. Kimmel

Richard C. Owen Publishers, Inc.
Katonah, New York

Meet The Author

Richard C. Owen Publishers, Inc.
PO Box 585
Katonah, New York 10536

Library of Congress Cataloging-in-Publication Data

Kimmel, Eric A.
    Tuning up : a visit with Eric Kimmel / by Eric A. Kimmel.
        p. cm.
    ISBN-13: 978-1-57274-822-4
    ISBN-10: 1-57274-822-2
    1. Kimmel, Eric A.—Juvenile literature. 2. Authors, American-20th
century—Biography—Juvenile literature. 3. Children's stories—Authorship—Juvenile
literature. I. Title.

PS3561.I4219Z476 2005
813'.54—dc22
[B]
                                                            2005048831

Color separations by Leo P. Callahan, Inc., Binghamton, New York

Printed in the United States of America

9   8   7   6   5   4   3   2   1

For more information about our collection of Meet the Author books
visit our website at www.RCOwen.com or call 800-336-5588.

To my grandson Blake and The Neighbors

Come on in. Sit yourself down.
I'll get my banjo and play something for you.

Jesse James was a lad who killed many a man.
He robbed the Glendale train.
He stole from the rich and he gave to the poor.
He'd a hand and a heart and a brain.

The Ballad of Jesse James is one of my favorite tunes.

I first heard the song when I was about seven years old.

One of my counselors at camp played it on his guitar.

It's a great song. It tells a story that makes you want to listen.

It makes you think of a lot of questions.

Who was Jesse James? What made him an outlaw?

How did he rob that train?

What happened to him afterwards?

That's how a good story starts. It doesn't spell everything out
for you. A good story gives you something to think about.
It raises as many questions as it answers.
A good story makes the listeners or the readers want to
stick around to the end. It makes them want to
hear it or read it again.

I grew up surrounded by stories from all over the world.
I'm a city boy originally. I grew up in Brooklyn, New York
in the 1950s. What a great place it was for a kid!
You could go anywhere by bike, bus, or subway.
For a fifteen-cent subway fare, you could go into
Manhattan and wander all over the city.
My friends and I went on an adventure every weekend.

We might go to the Planetarium to see the sky show, or to the Museum of Natural History to check out the dinosaurs. Or to the Metropolitan Museum of Art to visit the Egyptian mummies.

There was always something going on around Times Square and 42nd Street, the crossroads of the world.

I once shook hands with Eleanor Roosevelt. This great lady was the wife of one of the presidents of the United States. And one glorious afternoon we saw the singer and actress, Judy Garland, getting into a limousine. My friends and I stood on the corner, singing "Somewhere Over the Rainbow," the song she had made famous, and she waved to us as her car sped away.

When we got hungry, we'd head to my Uncle Al's place down on Canal Street for a soda and a sandwich.

We'd wind up the day by riding the ferry back and forth to Staten Island, taking in the sights of New York Harbor. The fare was only a nickel back then.

We had a whole day of adventures for less than seventy-five cents!

So how did I end up out west in Portland, Oregon?

New York City

Horace Greeley

From the time I was in high school, I spent my summers
working in New York City. My friend worked a few blocks
away. We'd meet at noon, sit on the benches in Greeley
Square, watch people go by, and eat our lunch beneath
the statue of Horace Greeley, the famous newspaper editor,
who once said, "Go West, young man." So I did.
My friend did too.

So choose where to sit carefully. It may change your life.

My growing up in a big city is the reason why
I write the way I do.

Many of the grandparents in my Brooklyn neighborhood
had come from other countries. I could walk down the street
and hear five different languages—Spanish, Italian, German,
Armenian, and Yiddish. The old people liked to sit outside
when the weather was good. They always had stories for any
kid who cared to listen and I got to hear stories from all over
the world.

Here is a picture of me and my brother at our neighbor
Sandra's birthday party. My brother is the toddler
on the left looking at his horn. I'm standing next to him.
Sandra's grandmother grew up in Puerto Rico.
She was a high school Spanish teacher and influenced
me to study Spanish. I grew up with Spanish.
I could hear Spanish being spoken through the walls
of our house. That's the reason many of my books have
Spanish or Latin American themes.

But here's the person who had the most influence on me.
This is my favorite picture of Grandma and me.
My brother is on the right. I'm on the left.

Here's another picture of Grandma
when she was much younger, when she
still lived in Europe.

She came to this country on a boat
in 1908, bringing with her many
treasures that are still in our family.

This is Grandma's Hanukkah menorah.
See how big and heavy it is.
I love those two brass lions.

I also have this little Hanukkah dreidel,
which has also been in the family
for close to a century.
It's the centerpiece of my dreidel
collection, which inspired my story
The Magic Dreidels.

Rynek — Ringplatz   Rynek — Ringplatz

Grandma's hometown in Europe was Kolomyya.
It's in Ukraine. My cousin went back a few years ago
to see what it was like. He says the only thing that's
changed from the old pictures is that the wagons now
have rubber tires. But to hear Grandma talk about her
hometown it was heaven.

Grandma never liked big cities. She loved the country:
fields, mountains, forests, rivers, and animals.
She especially loved dogs and horses.

Grandma liked bears, too. We always stopped to visit
the bears whenever we went to the zoo.

Grandma could handle a bear, which is why she inspired
the character Bubbe Brayna in *The Chanukkah Guest*.

THE
CHANUKKAH
GUEST

Eric A. Kimmel

illustrated by
Giora Carmi

What Grandma couldn't stand were cats.
She'd be horrified that we have three in our house
and that they sleep on the furniture.
Inky, Junior, and Puff. I definitely had them in mind
when I was working on *Three Samurai Cats*.
They are exactly like the cats in the story.

Tasha is our dog. She's a
soft-coated wheaten terrier.
She loves everybody.
Grandma would have liked her
a lot!

Grandma never went to school, but she spoke five languages and knew lots of stories—hundreds of stories!

But every time Grandma told a story, it was different.

Most of her stories were hair raising. Goblins, witches, ghosts and evil spirits always lurked in the shadows. What made these stories especially intense was that Grandma believed them.

"Every word is true. Dark corners are full of nasty creatures. They wait in the shadows to pounce on bad children who refuse to listen," she'd tell us.
So listen we did!

From Grandma's stories, I learned all sorts of signs and spells to ward off evil spirits. I spit three times to ward off the evil eye and I will never kill a spider. My wife thinks it's bizarre, but I can't help it.

The roots of *Hershel and the Hanukkah Goblins*
and many of my favorite books go back to those
childhood stories.

You have to write what you love. If you don't love your
own story, nobody else will.

Let's go down to the basement. I'll show you where I work.

This is my "Hobbit Hole." I like to surround myself
with my favorite things and am always looking for new
and interesting ones. Many of the objects have inspired
stories. I keep them near me while I write. They may give
me an idea.

Many of my stories begin with something I see.
Having an actual object to focus on helps a story get started.

Anansi is over here, on top of the bookshelf.

He came from Mexico. For some reason, he only has four legs.

Real spiders have eight. Anansi inspired me to write my book

Anansi and the Talking Melon.

I stared thinking about what might
happen if Anansi lost something
and had to find it. How would
he get it back? I had to think
hard to find an answer.

That's how a story begins.

19

 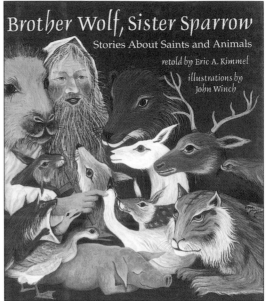

Here's Saint Francis and the Wolf of Gubbio.
Friends brought this little statue back from Italy.

Saint Francis lived in Italy during the Middle Ages.
He stopped a savage wolf from terrorizing the town by
making a deal with him. If the people of Gubbio fed the
wolf, the wolf promised to leave them alone. Saint Francis
and the wolf shook hands. From that day on, the wolf and
the people of Gubbio lived together in peace and friendship.
It's one of my favorite stories.

I used it in my book about saints and animals,
Brother Wolf, Sister Sparrow.

My fish tank is important to my writing.
When I get stuck, I clean the tank, or just watch the fish.

My musical instruments are important too: my harmonicas, my concertina, and my banjo. When I get stuck in my writing, or when I need a break, I pick up my banjo and practice a tune. Practicing clears my mind because I have to concentrate on what I'm doing. Sometimes, that's just what it takes to find the right idea to make a story work.

I can tell when my writing is going well. My banjo playing improves at the same time and I get a lot done.

The rest of the things in my "Hobbit Hole" are books, books, books! I love books. Books have been my best friends all my life. Some of them are for rescarch. Some are my own books.

I have a large collection from around the world. I love the pictures and can imagine stories that go with them.

The one thing about writing that most people may not realize is that writing comes out of your heart as well as your head. As I said before we went down to my "Hobbit Hole" in the basement, you have to love your story.

My original stories usually begin with an image:
a bear in the house; a spider stuck in a melon;
a Christmas tree with Hanukkah decorations on it.

Right now I have a great image in my mind of Santa Claus
in a red leather jacket riding a big motorcycle with an elf
and a bag of presents in the sidecar. I used to have a
motorcycle, so I have a soft spot for them.

Why is Santa on the motorcycle? Where is he going?
What happened to the reindeer?
I don't know. And until I figure out the answers,
I don't have a story.
Not yet.

Most of the real work is done before I write the first word.
I've always said that the hardest part of creating a book
isn't in the writing. It's in the thinking that goes on
before you write.

So it may look as if I'm just strumming my banjo,
watching fish, leafing through an old book,
staring into space, not doing much of anything.
But the truth is I'm working hard—I'm thinking!

Of course, thinking doesn't make a book.
You can't stop there.
Here are some letters and manuscripts from my files
to give you an idea of what the whole process looks like.

I'll work on a manuscript for months, rewriting the text, reworking the ideas until it is ready to send to the editor.

Editors choose the stories that are made into books.
If my editor likes the story, she'll have her own ideas
and suggestions, and write comments between the lines
and in the margins.

My editors have good ideas for making the story better.
I consider their suggestions seriously.
We talk about them.

I'll usually end up rewriting the story several times
until my editor and I are both satisfied that we've solved
all the problems, answered all the questions,
and turned a good story into an excellent one.

After that, the story goes to the artist who makes the pictures,
and I start working on another story.

Most people think the author and artist work closely together. Not true. That surprises many people who think I tell the artist what to draw. I look at it this way. If I've done my job, the artist will be able to imagine pictures by reading the words I've written. They may not be the pictures I had in my head, but that doesn't matter. Usually, they're better.

Now let's take a walk. I live in a famous neighborhood.
We're only a short walk from Klickitat Street.
Beverly Cleary, the author of all the books about
Henry Higgins, Beezus, and of course, Ramona,
grew up a few blocks away.

Grant Park is where so many events in those stories
happened. The Beverly Cleary Fountain is in the park.
My wife Doris and many of her friends helped plan
the construction of the fountain. Children from all over
the country collected dimes and quarters to raise money
to build the fountain.

Here are Ramona and Henry.

Do I want a statue erected for me? I'm always asked
that question, but I don't know if it is a good idea.
Walking through the park at night and encountering
a goblin from one of my books might be a little scary.

I don't really need a statue. Just knowing that children
all over the world enjoy my stories is enough for me.

Speaking of stories, it's time to get back to my writing.
So I'll say goodbye for now by picking up my banjo
and telling you the end of Jesse James' story.
It's not a happy one.

A man he thought was his friend shot Jesse dead
while he was hanging a picture on the wall.

Oh, Jesse had a wife to mourn for his life.
    Three children, they were brave.
But that dirty little coward who shot Mr. Howard
    Has laid poor Jesse in his grave.

Good, bad, happy, sad—I love a good story!

Your friend,
Eric A. Kimmel

Other Books by Eric A. Kimmel

Don Quixote and the Windmills; The Brass Serpent; The Erie Canal Pirates; Why the Snake Crawls On Its Belly; Website of the Cracked Cookies; Zigazak!; Website of the Warped Wizard; Robin Hook, Pirate Hunter; Gershon's Monster; Montezuma and the Fall of the Aztecs; Grizz!; The Two Mountains; The Rooster's Antlers; The Bird's Gift.

About the Photographer

Basil Childers enjoys a career in photography. His goal is to create images that educate, entertain, and inspire. From early life Basil Childers (born in Tulsa, Oklahoma) was fascinated with animals, nature, and with the photography and stories he read in *National Geographic*. At age 14 he purchased his first camera and practiced photography every day until he learned the skills needed to create amazing photographs. In college, Basil pursued biology and genetics, but chose instead to be a photographer so that he could document aspects of the world to show others. Basil's work spans many areas; dance, music, food, and architecture, but his favorite subjects have to do with environmental issues.

Acknowledgments

Photos on pages 3, 7, 10, 11, 13, top 14, bottom 17, top 19, 20, 22 courtesy of Eric A. Kimmel. Book cover on page 14 from *The Chanukkah Guest*, text copyright © 1988 by Eric A. Kimmel, illustrations copyright © 1990 by Giora Carmi. By permission of Holiday House. Book cover on page 17 from *Hershel and the Hanukkah Goblins*, text copyright © 1985 by Eric A. Kimmel, illustrations copyright © 1989 by Trina Schart Hyman. By permission of Holiday House. Book cover on page 19 from *Anansi and the Talking Melon*, text copyright © 1994 retold by Eric A. Kimmel, illustrations copyright © 1994 by Janet Stevens. By permission of Holiday House. Book cover on page 20 from *Brother Wolf, Sister Sparrow: Stories About Saints and Animals*, text copyright © 2003 retold by Eric A. Kimmel, illustrations copyright © 2003 by John Winch. By permission of Holiday House.

Meet the Author titles

Verna Aardema   *A Bookworm Who Hatched*
David A. Adler   *My Writing Day*
Frank Asch   *One Man Show*
Joseph Bruchac   *Seeing the Circle*
Eve Bunting   *Once Upon a Time*
Lynne Cherry   *Making a Difference in the World*
Lois Ehlert   *Under My Nose*
Denise Fleming   *Maker of Things*
Douglas Florian   *See for Your Self*
Jean Fritz   *Surprising Myself*
Paul Goble   *Hau Kola Hello Friend*
Ruth Heller   *Fine Lines*
Lee Bennett Hopkins   *The Writing Bug*
James Howe   *Playing With Words*
Johanna Hurwitz   *A Dream Come True*
Eric A. Kimmel   *Tuning Up*
Karla Kuskin   *Thoughts, Pictures, and Words*
Thomas Locker   *The Man Who Paints Nature*
Jonathan London   *Tell Me a Story*
George Ella Lyon   *A Wordful Child*
Margaret Mahy   *My Mysterious World*
Rafe Martin   *A Storyteller's Story*
Patricia McKissack   *Can You Imagine*
Laura Numeroff   *If You Give an Author a Pencil*
Jerry Pallotta   *Read a Zillion Books*
Patricia Polacco   *Firetalking*
Laurence Pringle   *Nature! Wild and Wonderful*
Cynthia Rylant   *Best Wishes*
Seymour Simon   *From Paper Airplanes to Outer Space*
Mike Thaler   *Imagination*
Jean Van Leeuwen   *Growing Ideas*
Jane Yolen   *A Letter from Phoenix Farm*

For more information about the Meet the Author books
visit our website at www.RCOwen.com or call 1-800-336-5588